Estuaries
Where Oceans and Rivers Meet

by Sheila Black

Table of Contents

Introduction

Picture yourself on a boat in a **marsh**. An otter swims by. Ducks and geese are flying overhead. On a nearby clump of grass, a blue heron watches the water for fish. This **habitat** is home to a great many kinds of plants and animals. It also provides important things, such as food and clean water, for humans. As we look at this marsh, we are reminded of how much life depends on the place where ocean and river meet—an estuary (ES-chew-er-ee).

Estuaries are wetlands such as marshes, bogs, swamps, and mudflats. An estuary is also a place where a river flows into an ocean. Fresh water and salt water mix in an estuary. Since estuaries are sheltered from the full force of the ocean, they are safe havens for many kinds of wildlife.

Estuaries form when rivers flow into ⊃ larger bodies of water on the eastern coast of the United States.

Area of
Detail

PENNSYLVANIA

Chesapeake
Bay

N.J.

Washington, D.C. ☆

DELAWARE

MARYLAND

VIRGINIA

ATLANTIC
OCEAN

⬆ Note how rivers widen as
they approach the ocean.

CHAPTER 1

Vital Habitats

What habitats can we find in estuaries? There are freshwater marshes where you might see moose and muskrats. In saltwater marshes ducks and herons usually can be found. There are mudflats where algae grow and clams make their homes. And there are shellfish beds filled with blue-black mussels and oysters. Sandy beaches and rocky shores are part of some estuaries too.

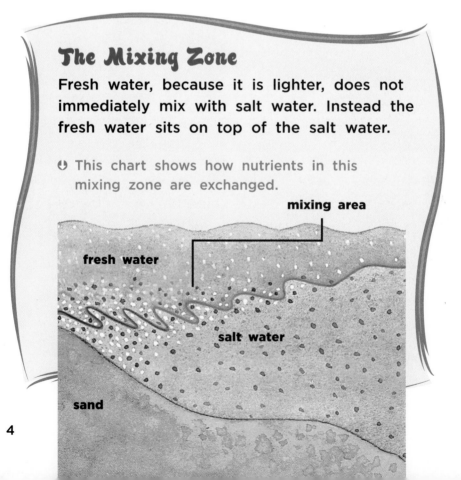

The Mixing Zone

Fresh water, because it is lighter, does not immediately mix with salt water. Instead the fresh water sits on top of the salt water.

☉ This chart shows how nutrients in this mixing zone are exchanged.

mixing area

fresh water

salt water

sand

Plankton

You need a microscope to see these tiny animals. But they are the basic food in an estuary. The more there are, the more food there is for larger animals. Dead plankton also help to form the rich bottom layer of estuaries. This makes food for plants.

This is a drawing of ➲ plankton as it would look magnified many times.

The mix of fresh and salt water in an estuary creates a rich "soup" that feeds all kinds of life. The ingredients of this soup come from both the land and the sea.

Rivers carry soil and minerals from the land into an estuary. This attracts sea creatures that need these nutrients. Sea plants grow well in estuary waters. These sea plants become food for fish and shellfish. This rich sea life, in turn, draws all kinds of birds and mammals. Why? They know they can count on getting a good seafood dinner!

CHAPTER 2

Estuary Plants

Plants that require lots of water grow easily in freshwater marshes. These plants are called **hydrophytes**. Many hydrophytes, like cattails and bulrushes, take root underwater. Others like algae never grow above the surface of the water. Some marsh water plants are "floaters." Their leaves float on the surface of the water. But their stems are underwater and rooted to the bottom. Water lilies and duckweed are plants that float.

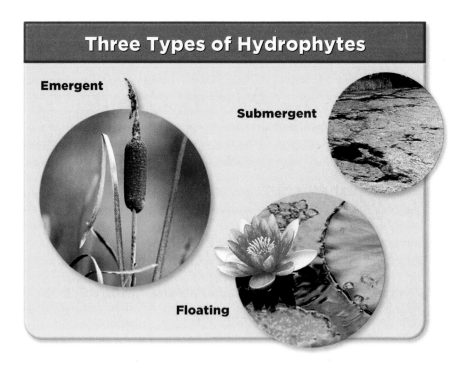

Three Types of Hydrophytes

Emergent

Submergent

Floating

Only a few plants can grow by the seashore. It is one of the hardest places in the world for plants to live, because moving tides hurt delicate plant leaves and stems. Also, plants have a hard time coping with salt water. When you put most plants in the sea, fresh water flows out of them and they die.

Spartina grass is hardy. It can grow in a mixture of fresh and salt water. It does this by sending out tough, wiry underground stems called **rhizomes**. These sprout into new plants. As these plants grow, they send out more underground stems. Soon a salt water marsh covered with spartina grass is formed. This grass gives food and shelter to animals that live there.

A Saltwater Survivor

The mangrove tree is one of the only trees in the world that can grow in salt water. Its clawed roots catch and hold soil. They help stop land **erosion** and build little islands where animals can live.

CHAPTER 3

Fish and Shellfish

Almost all the shellfish we catch and eat comes from estuary waters. Clams, oysters, mussels, and crabs can all be found in estuaries. Clams live in mudflats where mud builds up along the ocean shore. Oyster beds depend on the rich flow of food from estuary rivers and marshes. Crabs and shrimp use estuaries as nurseries because they provide young crabs and shrimp with plenty of food and a sheltered place to grow.

⟳ These men are harvesting shellfish in the Chesapeake Bay, the largest estuary in the United States.

An Oyster's Life

Oysters live for about twenty years, but they stop growing after five years.
As spats—or babies—they float, but they soon settle on a rock or reef. They then spend the rest of their lives in one place.

Fish live in estuaries too. Many of the fish we catch and eat spend their lives at sea. But they need fresh water to lay their eggs and give birth to the next generation. Salmon, trout, and striped bass all travel to estuaries to reach the fresh water they need to complete their life cycle. Even fish like flounder that are born in the open ocean need estuaries. They come to estuaries to get food and be sheltered from the wild ocean storms.

CHAPTER 4

Estuary Birds

Estuaries are important habitats for birds. Three quarters of the birds in the United States spend all or part of their lives in wetland estuaries. Why do birds live in estuaries? The plants and grasses give them shelter to nest in. There is always water to drink. And thanks to the mixing zone, there are many foods to eat such as insects, seeds, fish, and shellfish.

Great Blue Heron

Red-Wing Blackbird

Eastern Kingbird

Bald Eagle

10

🔊 White pelicans flock to the wetlands in Louisiana, near the Mississippi River and the Gulf of Mexico.

Some of the most beautiful birds are found in estuaries. The crane, the heron, and the egret live in estuary wetlands. Other birds visit estuaries on their yearly migrations, or journeys, between north and south. Ducks and geese fly south from Canada to Florida and on their way stop in freshwater and saltwater marshes. Songbirds visit too.

Adaptation is the way that an animal or plant copes with where it lives. Estuary birds such as ducks have oily waterproof feathers. These feathers keep them from getting too wet as they swim and dive for food. These feathers also help them stay warm.

CHAPTER 5

People and Estuaries

Estuaries are important to people, too. Half of the people in the United States live near an estuary. Yet estuaries only make up 11% of our land area.

Why are estuaries so popular? They provide food and water. There is also plenty to do near an estuary. People can sail, fish, and enjoy viewing all the wildlife. Since estuaries are near rivers and oceans, travel is easy.

Most big cities are near estuaries. Boston, Washington, D.C., and San Francisco are all big cities that were built on land that used to be an estuary marsh.

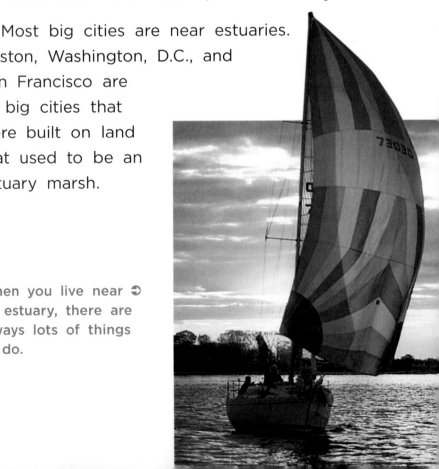

When you live near ⮕ an estuary, there are always lots of things to do.

⟳ People use waterways to take boats across a marsh. But waterways like this one keep marshes from getting the river floods they need.

Estuaries are good to people. But people are not always so good to estuaries. They drain land to build towns, farms, and factories. Plants and animals suffer. Farms and factories dump chemicals into estuaries. Sometimes the marshes get so dirty that there is not enough **oxygen** in the water. Plants and fish can't breathe. The marshes die.

People build canals or waterways through marshes too. This keeps them from getting flooded by rivers. Without river floods to bring in new soil, marshes often sink completely. There are places where an acre of land a day is lost this way.

Estuaries are always muddy. This is because mud and soil are always being washed into them by rivers. But too much mud can also cause big problems. Why? If there is too much mud in an estuary, it can smother shellfish. It can also turn clear water brown. When this happens many plants can't get enough light to grow. Too much mud can also cause the overgrowth of some plants like mangroves or marsh grasses. This pushes out other plants and animals.

CHAPTER 6

Save Our Estuaries

Today people see that our estuaries need help. In some estuaries plants and animals are dying. The number of fish and shellfish in some estuaries has fallen by two thirds.

Losing our estuaries causes other problems too. The marshes in estuaries are like giant sponges. They absorb water and store it. The marshes store water from heavy rainfalls too. This helps prevent floods. Estuary grasses and plants also trap dirt in the water. This way, they clean water that has been made dirty by factories and farms. This helps keep the drinking water clean. Estuaries give us many things. That's why across the United States, people are working to restore our estuaries.

This man is ➲ taking samples of water to be tested for pollutants.

They are listening to what scientists tell them. They are banning pesticides and other chemicals that hurt estuaries and their wildlife. They are digging holes, or diversions, in canals. These holes let marshes get flooded by rivers. This helps save wetlands. People are also creating preserves, or parks. There, people are not allowed to drain wetlands or fill in land to build towns or houses. This helps estuaries stay healthy.

Did You Know . . .

The Louisiana brown pelican is Louisiana's state bird. Forty years ago, it had almost died out. There were only 200 of them left. A pesticide called DDT was making the bird's eggs so thin that they broke before they could hatch. Lawmakers stopped farmers from using DDT. The brown pelican made a big comeback. Now there are over 10,000.

Conclusion

Preserving our estuaries is going to take a lot of work. But scientists are learning more about estuaries every day. People take part too. They volunteer for projects that keep watch over the estuaries. They report any changes they see to scientists. Here are some things that the volunteers do:

- They check water to make sure it is not polluted.
- They search for tagged animals and report their finding to scientists.
- They watch for invasive plants or animals, ones that do not naturally live in an estuary and could harm habitats of the wildlife that already live there.
- They teach adults and children facts about estuaries.

It's a Fact

The last Saturday in September is National Estuary Day. On that day you can tell people about estuaries. You can share what you learned in this book.

◖ Estuaries produce more plant and animal life each year than farmlands, forests, or grasslands of the same size.

Estuaries and all their wildlife are nature's gifts to us, ones that we need to preserve so that others may enjoy them in the future. Volunteers help out. Children can help too. They can learn about estuaries and share what they know with others. The more people know about estuaries, the more they will want to help them survive.

Glossary

adaptation *(a-dap-TAY-shuhn)* the process of changing to meet new conditions, or how animals change to cope with their homes or habitats *(page 11)*

erosion *(i-ROH-zhuhn)* the act or process of being worn away bit by bit by water or wind *(page 7)*

habitat *(HAB-i-tat)* the place where an animal or plant naturally lives and grows *(page 2)*

hydrophyte *(HIGH-droh-fight)* a plant that grows well in water *(page 6)*

marsh *(MAHRSH)* low, wet land *(page 2)*

oxygen *(OK-si-juhn)* a gas that has no color or smell *(page 13)*

rhizome *(RIGH-zohm)* an underground root system that lets new plants grow up from it *(page 7)*

Index

Comprehension Check

Summarize

Identify the following sentences as causes or effects. Then write the missing cause or effect for each.

Fresh water mixes with salt water.

People build apartment buildings near estuaries.

Estuary water is polluted.

The estuaries are flooded.

Think and Compare

1. Turn to page 14 in this book. What effect does river water have on an estuary? *(Identify Cause and Effect)*

2. If you could choose to live near any of the estuary habitats described in this book, which one would you pick? Why? *(Apply)*

3. Why is it important for volunteers to keep watch over estuaries? How do these volunteers help everyone in the United States? *(Evaluate)*